It [illegible]ut
The Client

LEE WATT

ISBN: 978-0-9925937-0-4

DEDICATION

This book is dedicated to Janine, whose example was the source of inspiration for the book.

CONTENTS

ACKNOWLEDGMENTS

Thank you Janine (not her real name) for giving me the inspiration for the concept of this book. My thanks to all of the wonderful hairdressers who have worked with me in my salons over the years, most importantly, all my past apprentices who allowed me to influence their journey in life by my guidance in their professionalism.

Thanks to all the hairdressers I have taught over the years. As I taught, I learned.

Thanks to my big brother Wayne for his command of the English language and his gentle encouragement as my editor.

1.

INTRODUCTION

The Story Behind This Book

I wrote this book because I believe we have a serious problem within our industry concerning our ability to service our clients with the respect and professionalism they deserve. I get very disturbed by the lost opportunities for business growth in the hairdressing industry, well, any industry I suppose, because of a lack of respectful service and client care. So many opportunities are lost due to bad manners and a poor understanding of business etiquette.

A good hairdresser is one who retains a significant client base while working to continue building that client base.

This is achieved by genuine Client Care.

Client Care is all about what I call Salon etiquette. Client Care encompasses good manners, good hairdressing and excellent service.

The hairdressing service industry demands an enormous commitment: a commitment to please others, a commitment to genuinely care for our clients, and then you have to do *good hair* too.

We love to be involved in the hairdressing industry, because we love doing hair and we generally love people. Some of us can create rapport and effectively cater for every personality quite naturally. Others have to learn the art of Client Care.

Recognise that you have fantastic power as a professional hairdresser. You can change people's lives with your skill as a hairdresser. You can turn a seriously unhappy person into a confident and well groomed person who is now a very happy individual. A visit to the hairdresser should be a joyful experience with a fantastic outcome. You have the ability to change lives for the better. You may not realise this, but when people walk past the door of your salon they see confident, well groomed hairdressers having fun and they admire and respect your ability.

Imagine if we understood our power, understood what it is to service our clients professionally, understood that our clients want and need our care. In fact, most clients are begging for professional help to assist them in maintaining their hair. The art of doing hair is a complete mystery to some, and they really need and appreciate the help of the hairdresser and the advice we offer.

Imagine what a difference that would make to our day. How as hairdressers we would take complete control of our clients' needs. Our clients would love us for our complete professionalism in caring for their hair, and all of their home hair care needs as well.

Many years ago I was taught how to totally care for my clients by one very special girl. She was the epitome of professional client care. She was the best money taker I have ever employed and yet she wasn't the best hairdresser I have ever employed. She maintained her personality and character while abandoning any thought of self in order to take care of her clients.

I now recognise that she had a shy personality, and so she never talked about herself. She knew to talk only to the client about the client. They loved her for that.

Her clients had such a wonderful time with her in the salon. They had every service she ever suggested and they didn't seem to mind that their hair was shorter on one side than the other. So calm and focused was she that it probably never occurred to her that hair shorter on one side than the other was only a good thing when it was intentional. Her clients loved this hairdresser as a friend and a daughter.

At Christmas, Easter and birthdays the back room of the salon looked like Myers; five birthday cakes and each one accepted with graceful astonishment, as if it were the only cake she had seen in her life, let alone that day. There were Easter eggs enough to fill Myers' order Australia wide, and enough Christmas presents to make any tree proud.

All this was because she demonstrated the greatest attention to salon etiquette and client care. She showered her clients with her undivided attention. She believed in her clients, and they rewarded her efforts with their devotion to her.

She left my employ to embark on her own business and naturally, she was very successful. Janine understood the art of salon etiquette and client care.

What do I mean by salon etiquette?

Salon etiquette is good manners in business; how to make other people feel good by the care and attention you give them.

“People will forget what you said, they will forget what you did but they will never forget how you made them feel.” - (Maya Angelou.)

The life of a busy hairdresser is very demanding. However, it is a million times more rewarding than the life of a not-so-busy hairdresser.

You may think that the busy hairdresser is the best stylist, but the only difference between a busy hairdresser and a not-so-busy hairdresser is client care and salon etiquette.

OK ... Let’s start at the very beginning.

2

THE WELCOME

First Impressions

"There is no second chance to make a first impression." - (Will Rogers)

Imagine you are having a party at home and the doorbell rings. You rush excitedly to the door and fling it open with a big smile on your face. You are so pleased to be greeting your first guests. You welcome them into your home. You take their coat and bag. You make sure they are comfortable. You get them a drink and then you rush back to the front door and do it all over again for the next arrivals. You then introduce the first guests to the next guests and you get the new guests comfortable and ... do you see where I am going with this?

Greeting guests at home is no different from greeting customers in your salon. Of course you need to make a fuss of them. You invited them into your salon didn't you? Sure you did, when you started that marketing campaign for your business. You invited clients to come to your salon because it was the BEST. You made loads of promises in that marketing campaign too. You promised the best *this* and the best *that*, and how you would take care of them as a client - didn't you?

Well this is your opportunity to live up to the promises. The clients are arriving like the invited guest they are.

Are you ready?

Start the overture, raise the curtain. You're on!

She walks briskly into your salon. She's standing at the desk. She wants attention, and she needs to be acknowledged.

You see her. You acknowledge her with a smile and a nod.

You excuse yourself from your client. You wait for your client to excuse you, and you walk towards her, maintaining eye contact while you have a pleasant look on your face. You are going to say "Yes" to whatever she asks of you.

She has high expectations because she's seen your clever advertising, and is looking forward to a good experience.

Hairdresser: "How may I help?"

Client: "Could I have a haircut?" (Do not assume she means NOW.)

Hairdresser: "Certainly when would you like it?"

Client: "Is there any chance of right away?"

Now, as you walk towards that client you would know

the availability of the operators in your salon, and be ready for every situation. What if she does want a haircut right now? Who is available, and if not right now, when would the first available appointment be?

Why do hairdressers scowl at the appointment book or screen? There may be three operators in that salon doing very little, and the one at the desk will stare at the appointment book/screen. Then she will look back into the salon, look at her watch, look back at the book, look at the client, (like she's hoping she may have changed her mind) look back into the salon and finally say discouragingly "NO. We can't do it for half an hour."

Hmmmm! No ten out of ten for that welcome.

OK. Action replay!

Client: "Is there any chance of right away?"

Hairdresser: "Absolutely! Can you give us 20 minutes?"

Client: "Yes, that's fine."

Hairdresser: "Excellent, would you like to go shopping or have a coffee here with us while you wait?" (Oh! You have invited her in. That's nice.)

Seat her, organise the coffee, arrange for some magazines and let her get comfortable in your salon. Now go back to the appointment book or screen and complete the paper work.

Your priority is to get that client into your salon environment and to get her comfortable, so don't fiddle with the paper work at the desk first.

OK. What if you really can't do it in the next hour/ day?

Client: "Is there any chance of right away?"

Hairdresser: "We would really love to look after your hair. (Pause, look at the client.) We have two appointments available for today. One at 2:30 pm and another at 4:00 pm. Would either of these times suit you?"

TAKE 2. Hairdresser: "We would really love to look after your hair, however we are fully booked today. We do have some available appointments tomorrow. What time is most suitable for you tomorrow?"

The client needs to hear from you that you really want to look after her. Remember that you are flattered that she walked past 15 salons to front up to yours. You have to admire her intelligence in choosing you.

Thank her: "Thank you for choosing our salon."

3

BREAKING THE ICE

Be Gentle

Have you ever arranged to meet friends for dinner with you as the first to arrive at the restaurant? The surroundings are not familiar to you. As you are seated at your table all alone and on show, you get to feel most uncomfortable until your friends arrive.

Similarly, if this is the very first time the client has ever been to your salon, she is very unfamiliar with the place, and feeling a little anxious. So you will need to take great care with her.

The salon is very familiar to the people who work within it. They seem to spend half their life in that salon. Every salon operates in a different manner. Some salons like to do a consultation at the styling area before the hair is shampooed. Some like their clients to go straight to the shampoo area.

Firstly, invite your client into the salon by looking her directly in the eye and in a calm manner say: "Welcome Mary, my name is Jane. Would you please come this way."

Now walk with her, and indicate exactly which chair you would like her to use by holding the back of the chair and again looking directly at the client say: "Would you please sit here Mary", holding the chair until she is settled.

I know this may seem a bit obvious to some. However, would you be surprised at the poor results if your invitation is mumbled, and no eye contact is made? The client may not have heard your instruction to "Follow me." or worse, "This way". Perhaps she even doubted you were talking to her because you didn't look at her when you mumbled something. You just took off into the salon, and left the client standing, confused and embarrassed.

Are you off to a good start here with your client care and salon etiquette? I think not!

Remember she is in unfamiliar territory at first, and once she is settled and can get a good look around, she will begin to feel more comfortable.

If someone else is directing your client for you, make sure that they are the one to introduce you to your client. Instruct your staff to take time to carefully introduce the new client to the salon. They are playing the host at their very own party and need to ensure that the client feels comfortable and acknowledged and is being introduced to the people who are going to have contact with her hair during her visit to the salon.

4

ESTABLISH RAPPORT

Know Your Client's Name

Calling your client by her name often during the service is a great compliment and also a great way to relax your client. This is another very important element in salon etiquette and client care.

As your client moves around the salon for each service, be sure to introduce your client to the operator who is going to shampoo for you, or the colourist or the beauty therapist.

Each operator who has contact with the client should be introduced or introduce themselves.

If you can train yourself to remember your client's name, you will certainly win her over next time she enters the salon and you can address her by name. She now feels very important and appreciated. It is probably the greatest compliment you could pay her. You are on the way to winning a client for life!

5

THE CONSULTATION

Listen

It's all about the client, not about you. You will make the best impression on your client if you just refrain from talking, and concentrate on listening.

Now I know how this feels. You want to appear knowledgeable and inspirational. Your head is spinning with ideas, and you are looking at the colour, the texture, and the shape of the client's hair in front of you.

Your brain is scrambling, trying to think of what you are going to do to make this head of hair look a whole lot better. You are wondering how much money this client has to spend.

At the beginning of the consultation, the client was explaining what she wanted done. All that time your head was spinning. You did not hear a word the client had to say. Now you are busy mouthing off about what you are going to do, how you want to do it, what colour it should be, where it needs a bit of texture taken out of it, what the plan is for the future, and then how much it is all going to cost, and you ask: "How do you feel about that?"

I'll tell you how she feels about that:

Sick to death of going to hairdressers who DO NOT LISTEN to any of what she said she wanted. And that's not the only thing she is sick of. While you tell her about how fabulous you are going to make her look with completely the opposite to what she said she wanted, you have been standing behind her talking to her through the mirror, and checking yourself out while you're at it!

Eventually she gives up, totally exasperated as she ticks off another experience she would rather not have had, and settles in to cop whatever you dish up, while living in hope that some semblance of good hairdressing is about to take place.

What if you had actually listened?

Really listened.

What if you sat with her at eye level while you gradually got to understand where she was coming from and how she wanted her hair to look?

Only after you clarified with her what she wanted, do you come in with any of your suggestions and finally a quote for the whole procedure.

Here's how your consultation should be conducted:

You need to ask open ended questions as opposed to closed ended questions.

An open ended question is a question that requires

more than a “yes” or “no” answer.

Open Example: “So Jayne, tell me how you feel about your style at the moment?”

Now Jayne has to talk to you and tell you her frustrations, likes and dislikes about her hair.

Closed Example: “Jayne are you happy with your style at the moment?”

This question will get you a “yes” or “no” answer, and you need more information to make a style suggestion for Jayne.

Following is a list of some open ended questions you might like to emulate to make your consultations more successful and to take control of your client. You need to be the one in control of this consultation because it takes a lot more time if your client wants to tell you about what Aunty Jean thinks of her hair and how it is just like her brother David’s hair before he married Alice .... Blah, blah, blah.

By having a series of questions that you feel comfortable asking, that you are very familiar with, you will be able to stay in control of the conversation. If you feel your client is giving too much useless information you can just nicely ask the next question.

Now your client is not going to be offended if you interrupt her in mid-stream because she is talking about herself, while you are listening for the important information and deciding how you are going to fulfill all your client’s needs.

Question 1. “So Jayne, tell me how you feel about

your style at the moment?"

Question 2. "Jayne, if there was one thing you would like to change about your colour, what would it be?"

Question 3. "How often do you shampoo your hair Jayne?"

Question 4. "How long would you like to grow your hair?"

Question 5. "What products and appliances do you use when you do your hair at home?"

Question 6. "Jayne what is your preference regarding the length of your hair?"

Now let me tell you that you do have to practice asking these questions out loud. Because you need to hear how they will sound to your client so they must be asked with "feeling" not as if you have learned them off by heart. When you think you have enough information, you just ask the next question.

You need a question that covers every aspect of the consultation.

1. Style
2. Colour
3. Length
4. Home maintenance

Some questions can lead you to a great discussion, and that's perfectly OK if they're giving you good information. If not, move on to the next question.

Be sure to check if she has any concerns about her scalp health as well. This allows a conversation about very personal subjects like dandruff, or itchy scalp or any other debilitating scalp conditions.

Success is all about the "Three Ps". Preparation, preparation and preparation. By asking a series of targeted questions, you have gathered all the information you need to be successful.

I still hear hairdressers who ask that bloody awful question: "Much off?" I can assure you that they must be very bored people who have definitely chosen the wrong profession.

6

THE QUOTE

Everyone relaxes after the "Money Conversation"

I live by the mantra: "People accept almost anything if told in advance."

Would you buy a fashion item without knowing how much it was going to cost?

What about car insurance? Ever bought car insurance without finding out how much it was going to cost?

A quote before proceeding with any work will free up the mind of the stylist as well as the client. I don't know many stylists (other than salon owners) who like to take money for making beautiful hair. They would rather just do it all for free. They seem to think that the commercialism of it all undermines their creativity. If the money discussion is out of the way, the hairdresser and the client can now relax, and the client can really get to enjoy being in your salon.

It's horrific to hear scary stories of a client first receiving a quote for the services. The session proceeds. More services are suggested with no charge mentioned. The client agrees, thinking "It will be nice to have a beautiful treatment", only to discover when they get to the front desk that there are charges for all those beautiful extras.

The quote you give her for the work you believe will fulfill her wants and needs may or may not be acceptable to her. She may decide not to go ahead at the moment with various recommendations. She is however, now fully informed and can relax and enjoy your service and professionalism without any unknowns, or fear of getting to the register to be asked to fork out enough to purchase a small block of land in Switzerland.

7

THE ART OF SELLING

Give Out Good Information

I know most hairdressers would rather walk over cut glass than "sell retail", probably because they see themselves as professionals and not sales people.

Well I believe that you are being very professional when you discuss the needs of your client and her home hair care routine.

Your client probably doesn't have the foggiest idea about how to look after your clever art work (her hair-style). She will see you opening up little jars of stuff to put in her hair. She sees the way you play with her hair to achieve the look you are wanting, yet she is at a loss as to how to achieve that effect herself.

Here is the answer to help you have that conversation with your client.

Tell.

Don't sell.

Just tell your client what she should be doing to look after the health of her hair.

Break it up into three categories.

1. Shampoo and conditioner.
2. Treatments.
3. Styling products.

Tell your client how you are going to advise her by saying something like: "Today I want to tell you about what I think you need to do to look after your hair at home, and I will also show you what products you need."

Then say: "Please don't feel that you have to buy anything, just let me show you what I think you need."

Show and tell.

Show your client the products and tell her how you would use them. Don't rave on for hours about the range and don't tell her that you use that product (she doesn't care what you use). Just calmly tell her about the range you are proposing that will fix any concerns she may have about her hair. In consultation, that is one of the most important questions to ask.

"What concerns you the most about your hair?"

Once the client has told you what her concerns are she has now given you the right and responsibility to address those concerns.

Imagine if she told you her concerns about her hair and you just said "Gee that sounds tough. Poor you."

You are her hairdresser. She needs you to help her look after her hair.

Tell her everything she needs to know to give her a

fighting chance of getting her hair to look as good as you are able to.

No need to labour the point by repeating yourself. Just give out good honest information. Tell the truth, and don't concern yourself about whether she will buy all or any of your recommendations.

She will need to see the products though, so I suggest you show the product while you give a brief explanation of how each product is used. It is then easy to just ask the question: "Would you like to take anything with you today?"

Prepare for her answer which will be one of the following:

1. "Yes." - Excellent.
2. "No." - Don't take it personally, and don't try to change her mind.
3. "Maybe." - More information required.

Now write down the things she needs and give her the list of her home hair care needs.

Help your client to manage her hair at home. It makes your job much easier if her hair is well maintained and she is not wasting her time wandering the aisles of the supermarket trying to find the elixir of life for her hair. You are giving excellent client care.

To demonstrate the point further, let me tell you about a promotion we did in a salon I owned. We had a 'Mystery Client' Promotion where six women were each given $100 to come to our salon to have their hair done. A girlfriend of mine selected the clients so that even I did not know who was a mystery client for the duration of the promotion.

At a staff meeting, prior to the start date of the promotion, I explained what was going to happen for the next two weeks of this promotion and how the mystery clients had been told to book in for a cut and blow dry. I told my staff that my friend had told the mystery clients that they could spend the whole $100, but only if they were offered extra services or products by the hairdresser and only if they wanted to have those services or products.

At the end of the promotion we invited the mystery clients to tell us about their experience in our salon. The most amazing thing happened during the promotion. My staff were sure that almost every client they touched was the mystery client over the two week period. Conversations in the back room of the salon were hilarious, with each staff member saying things like, "I've got one…I bet this is one of the mystery clients, she is having every service I suggest."

The offshoot of this whole experience was that our takings went up by 20 – 30% in that two week period, which made everyone very aware that we were not completely servicing our existing clientele and we were missing out on a lot of business. One of the reasons was that we underestimated the spending power of our clientele. When that restriction was mentally taken away from us because we thought every client had $100 to spend in our salon, our business increased. We were not judging people.

Our meeting with the mystery clients following the promotion was also a lot of fun when the real mystery clients were revealed, and their feedback was mostly positive. They loved the attention they had received, and their new styling products. Most of the mystery clients spent much more than the $100 they were given.

It was a great promotion and I think we got a lesson we didn't expect, with the increase in our turnover. It gave my stylists a lot of confidence to forget about the money and concentrate on fulfilling all of the needs of their clients.

8

THE RECORDS

Write It Down

Keeping good client records saves a lot of anxiety as you won't need to try to remember what you did last time. It's all there in front of you, and makes you look like the true professional that you are.

Remember that brilliant idea you had at the clients last visit? She has been thinking about it ever since, and if the school fees weren't due she would have had it done when you suggested it.

She is back and she wants that brilliant idea now, but you can't remember what the brilliant idea was. Now your head is really spinning as she tries to explain what it was that was so brilliant.

Embarrassing isn't it? Because you are just not getting it. She knows it. You know it, and she is disappointed because she has been really looking forward to it. She has been explaining it to her girlfriends, telling them that she is going to have a new cut or colour when it's time for her next appointment.

But you can't remember!!

It's been six weeks and 200 clients since her last visit!

Of course you can't remember!!

That's what records are for. You would have needed to record your brilliance, so that you can re-suggest that service, even if she hasn't been dreaming about it since her last appointment.

Record everything! All the recommendations you made with regard to her home hair care as well. You don't want to recommend one brand as gold, and during the very next visit, rave about another brand of home hair care.

Keeping good records saves a lot of angst and gives you that really professional look. You appear to remember what you said last time, having reviewed her records before she came for her appointment.

Now you are a hero, and a good student of client care and salon etiquette.

9

HONESTY

Admit Your Mistakes

The old saying "Honesty is the best policy" really does carry some weight when dealing with clients. It can happen in the best salons. The colour you told the client you were working towards is nothing like the colour she has sitting on her head at completion.

What are you going to do?

Pretend it hasn't happened and blow dry like mad to get her out of there before she realises she is screaming orange instead of the promised caramel colour?

Dry the front first so that it doesn't look so ORANGE?

Babble a lot so she can't get a word in?

Tell her it is "lovely" and really "suits" her?

No, no, no!

You are going to be HONEST. It is the wrong colour. It is not what she said she wanted. It is not what you told her it was going to look like. It is wrong!

Here's what to do:

Pull up a chair and say. "Mary, I'm so sorry. I am not completely happy with your colour."

Explain what is wrong with the colour.

Apologise.

Provide a solution.

Ask for her permission to go ahead with your solution.

"The colour is way too warm for our target colour. I do apologise. I will need to tone it down, and I can do that for you now.

I'm sorry that it's going to take more of your time. Is that OK with you?"

Now please, do not try to make yourself look smart by explaining in great detail the technicalities of correcting the screaming orange and making it caramel. She doesn't want to hear it because she understands none of it and she just wants her hair the colour you promised in the first place.

You will annoy the daylights out of her when you start rambling on about how you need to add a colour with a blue base, and you going to use C8 blended with a bit of C7 to give it a bit more depth. All she hears is "blue" and "depth" and now she is thinking she is going to end up dark blue, and she is very uncomfortable, and she is embarrassed, possibly more for you than herself, because she really, really wanted you to succeed.

Say as little as possible and do a lot.

Do not try to blame a bad batch of colour.

Do not blame the medication she is on.

Do not blame anyone or anything.

Do not try to make a joke of it.

Acknowledge the fact that you have inconvenienced your client and fix it.

10

DON'T GET TOO EXCITED!

Could I suggest keeping your voice at an even volume and speed when you want to develop a good relationship with your client at the first meeting. Best not to frighten the client.

You don't have to be an all singing all dancing ball of energy and witty remarks when you are first introduced to your client. She would like to have a very earnest conversation with you about her hair and so doesn't need you to thrust your sparkling personality in her face. She can get to know you better as your relationship, trust and respect develops, helped by the professional attitude you display toward your wonderful new client.

11

THE COLOUR CHART

Keep It To Yourself

The colour chart is a complete mystery to the client. She does not need to be shown the colour chart. She does not need that full blown technical explanation of which colour you are going to mix with which colour to achieve that which to her eye, looks nothing like the colour she actually wants.

Good colourists never show the colour chart to the client. A good colourist does not even need a colour chart.

Resist the temptation to "show off" your knowledge, and keep your colour chart to yourself.

12

TALKING HEADS

That's Just Rude

Two staff enjoying a conversation over the head of the client is a guaranteed way to alienate your client.

Your client came to your salon principally to have her hair done, relax and feel pampered, and to have a bit of special time for herself.

She doesn't want to hear about your boyfriend or what you did on the weekend or any other useless gossip.

On a recent visit to the hairdresser, I had my head down ready for the first snip, and my hairdresser said; "Oh by the way, the boss has been in, and I got the approval for my holidays." I was thinking; "Is she talking to me?" Her work mate answered by stating how happy she was for my hairdresser. They then began a long discussion about who would be working over Christmas.

I was being completely ignored.

Not an example of good client care.

Your client may however, enjoy talking about herself.

Most people love to talk about themselves. Just be careful that your "conversation starters" are not of too personal a nature.

"Are you married Adele?" could lead you into serious trouble if she happens to be on her third bitter divorce.

"What are you doing on the weekend?" is another very personal question. Why would she want to tell you what she is doing on the weekend? She may have a secret rendezvous planned, or worse still, absolutely nothing planned and is not feeling good about it.

Your conversation should be all about your client, predominately her hair, and don't assume that she must have something special on tonight to go to the trouble of having her hair done.

If you can't think of anything to say, it is best to say nothing.

Your client deserves your undivided attention, and sometimes the "chat, chat, chat" can just be a bit much for someone who wants to relax, so just concentrate on what you are doing.

I was once witness to the most amazing situation in a salon. The hairdresser was really going for it with her conversation about whatever while she was busily snipping away. She was really on a roll, and loved checking herself out in the mirror while she went on and on. Eventually, the client whose facial expression was becoming increasingly alarmed said "STOP! STOP!"

The hairdresser stopped, looking like she had been

slapped!

"What?" she says.

"Look what you've done. I said I only wanted a little bit off. Now you've gone and cut it too short. Look, I can hardly grab a piece of hair, it's so short!"

You are not going to believe what the hairdresser did!

She slammed her scissors and comb down on the work bench, put her hands on her hips and in a rather hurt tone, said: "I haven't finished yet."

Obviously in the client's mind, she should have finished about ten minutes ago. There is now no way known to mankind, to get that client to come back to that hairdresser, or to that salon ever again.

This is an amazing example of a lost opportunity. She had a client and now she has lost a client.

Salons spend a fortune on advertising to get new clients, but if they still had every client they ever laid hands on, they would never have to look any further.

Your "kept client" ratio could be dramatically increased by the good hair that you do, and the good client care that you give, and not necessarily in that order.

13

GETTING MARRIED

Shut Up!

OK. To all the hairdressers who are getting married or going overseas soon…SHUT UP!!

I understand that this is a very special time for you. I understand that it takes a lot of organisation to pull off the most fabulous wedding or overseas holiday, and, as your fellow worker, I sure as heck don't want to hear about it all day long as you tell client after client the tedious details of your upcoming event.

I know it's all fresh to your client, however your fellow stylists are ready to climb the walls as you repeat your clever planning one more time with feeling.

Honestly, don't start in the first place. STOP talking about yourself! You are not the most fascinating person in existence and your wedding plans will send your fellow stylists to the funny farm before they finally make it to the wedding.

OMG! They have just realised they will have to go through the honeymoon 84,000 times as well!

STOP IT!

14

WHERE'S THE BABY?

Please, Don't.

Please resist the temptation to talk baby talk to your elderly clients.

Those sing-song cutsie-pie "baby talk" questions, mostly committed by the younger members of the salon staff when questioning an older client about whether they would like a cup of tea:

"Would you like a cup of tea Doreen?"

The young stylist asking the question sounds like she is putting on her baby voice to ask a perfectly normal question to a perfectly capable and normal woman.

I bet Doreen would like to slap the baby talker.

Be very careful that you are not sounding condescending in your conversation. Those who appear elderly to you, do not seem that way to another, and anyway, why are you talking to the elderly client like she is a child? She is a mature woman. She chose to be a client of the salon and she has made a very intelligent decision to come to your salon. Don't make her regret that decision by treating her disrespectfully.

15

BEEN TO THE HAIRDRESSER?

Colour On Your Collar As Well As Your Hair

Maybe it is not the haircut your friend is remarking on when she asks if you have just been to the hairdresser. Maybe it's the fact that you have bits of hair stuck in your ears and all over the back of your skirt.

Please clean up your clients before they leave the salon to parade down the high street. Make sure there are no bits of hair stuck to them or their clothing, and make sure they still have both eyebrows on and that their make up is intact.

Obviously it shouldn't be there in the first place, but please make sure that they don't have colour on the skin around their hairline or on their clothes. Your clients are your walking advertisement, and should not look like they have just come from the hairdresser with evidence like attached debris, missing eyebrows or stained clothes.

Be very careful to wrap your client well before any colour service as well because she doesn't want the collar of her blouse the same colour as her hair.

16

I DIDN'T WANT A HAIRCUT!

When I ask almost anyone to describe their most memorable visit to the hairdresser the most common memory is about having too much hair cut off. That, coupled with the fact that the hairdresser chatted about herself while she chopped and chopped.

As a hairdresser you have surely experienced this yourself.

Your fellow stylist suggests she will just take the dead ends off your hair. Your long hair has soon been cut back to shoulder level because she HAD to do it! "It was all broken and split and the hair wasn't any good anyway."

Your client feels just like you do when you have had a haircut that is too short or maybe not too short, just not what she asked for. She feels pissed off and angry, and she will never return.

I phoned my Mother one day.

"How are you going Mum?"" I asked.

"Good" she said. "I've been to the hairdresser today,

and I'm just sitting here trying to find a piece of hair on my head longer than three centimeters."

Luckily, she has a good sense of humour.

Be gentle with those scissors. It's better to take just a little and have the client return, than to have YOUR way and cut the hair because you thought it necessary.

You can build a whole business around helping people to grow their hair. Instead of asking how much the client wants taken off their hair (when they really don't want anything cut off), why don't you just ask them; "How long would you like to grow your hair?"

Now you can explain that you are just going to "polish" the ends off (that means take just the smallest amount off the length), and that if you promise to do this, she has to promise to come back every six weeks to have the ends "polished off". She also has to promise to do a conditioning treatment on the hair every week at home to nourish and strengthen the hair so that it won't break and split.

Now you are both happy. She gets to keep her hair, and you get to keep a new client who just loves to tell everyone about her fabulous hairdresser.

17

STARTING YOUR OWN BUSINESS

You're going out on your own.

Congratulations! You are going to open your very own hairdressing salon.

It is NOT OK to tell all your clients on the side where you are going to open and when.

It is NOT OK to slip them your new business card. Apart from the ethical considerations of stealing your employer's customers, trust yourself and your abilities, and maintain your dignity. Believe me, your clients will find your new salon if they want to. They will beat a path to your door if you have been exercising good client care throughout your career.

18

WORKPLACE DISTRACTIONS

The salon is a sanctuary and a place of business. It should not therefore attract visitors who have no intention of using the services on offer. Those that just pop in for a chat are not welcome.

Your mobile phone should be on "silent". You can check your phone during the breaks. It's not important. Some ring-tones can really ruin the conversation. In this age of social media and addiction to mobile communication, perhaps you can even consider asking your clients to put their phones on silent, so they can really enjoy the experience in your salon. Just make sure it's worth their while staying incommunicado for their visit.

Never have discussions with representatives within earshot of your clients. They have no need to know that if you buy a trailer load of bleach you get a trailer load of developer to go with it and that would make it $2.58 per application. Professional representatives will make an appointment with you, and you will give them the courtesy of taking that time off the floor to listen to whatever that representative has to tell you.

Personal phone calls on the land line are a big NO-NO!

19

BAD PRACTICE

Please Avoid

Don't take your regular customers for granted.

As hairdressers we have to be very careful not to become too familiar with our clients. It's OK to have a close friendly relationship with our clients, however I wouldn't recommend socialising with your clients if you want to be able to maintain a professional relationship. Think about your relationship with your doctor, your accountant and your dentist. Do you want to socialise with any of these professionals? I think not. Keep your personal life and your professional life completely separate.

Here's an example of taking a customer for granted:

My friend Nicole was telling me about her recent visit to her hairdresser. She had been a client of this hairdresser for about four years. On this particular visit, Nicole was kept waiting for an extraordinary period of time. Her hair had been coloured and now she sat patiently waiting for her haircut and blow dry. The minutes ticked by, and eventually the owner of the salon came over to Nicole. "I apologise for the delay, Nicole. We have a colourist from a hair company here to show us a new colour. The model's hair is so long and thick, it's taking an age to get the colour on the model. We'll be with you shortly, OK?"

"Shortly" turned into "not so shortly", and with each passing minute Nicole was becoming more and more annoyed. The owner returned a couple of times to apologise again. Eventually the owner offered to cut and blow dry Nicole's hair for her because her usual stylist was involved in the colour trial with the model and the colourist.

Now you may ask, what's wrong with that? The salon owner did explain what the hold up was and did offer to finish Nicole's hair.

I'll tell you what is wrong with the situation. This book is called "It's All About the Client", and in this case the client was made to sit and wait, while preference was given to the colour demonstration the salon was having.

The solution is not to let a company do a colour demonstration during working hours and also, when having a colour demonstration, not to choose a model with the worst and hardest head of hair to colour (just to test the ability of the company colour consultant).

It is not good enough that the owner of the salon apologised. The situation should never have occurred in the first place, and everything else should have taken second place to the client.

Nicole's experience left her with a very bad taste in

her mouth, and a haircut that was not what she wanted. She preferred the work of her usual stylist.

Your clients have a life too, and when they decide to come to your salon they have allocated a certain amount of time for that event. They want to move on to the other elements of their very busy day, and if you hold them up you will start to dissolve your relationship with your client.

Having to wait for an extended period could be the straw the breaks the camel's back. Perhaps the next time you see that client, she is walking around with some other hairdresser's style sitting on her head.

You had her. Don't lose her.

20

HYDRAULIC CHAIRS

"Going Down."

Let your client know you are going to lower the chair before you plummet her four floors at breakneck speed. Seriously, she could bite her tongue.

21

TIMERS

Countdown To Disaster

Do not keep the timer in front of the client. It worries the heck out of her, especially if no one comes when it goes off and she is left to imagine all those little packets of foil falling to the floor with her hair in them, as the minutes tick by unattended.

22

THE LAUGHING STOCK

"Don't Make Fun Of Me."

A disturbing story related to me was that of a client who left her last salon because they were teasing her.

Now I will forgive you for thinking "what sort of neurotic client is that?"

Apparently she tripped and fell when entering the salon one day. She has a fabulous sense of humour and laughed along with everyone else after it was established that she wasn't seriously hurt. The problem was that every time she entered the salon afterwards, (three times in all) the staff made a big fuss of taking her arm and carefully leading her into the salon, making jokes like "careful as we go", and everyone had a good laugh. This she found too hard to bear because she was embarrassed when she fell, and did not wish to relive the experience every time she entered the salon.

It is very bad manners to repeatedly remind the client of her unceremonious encounter with the floor, in a weak attempt to cover your own discomfort.

23

THE TELEPHONE AND APPOINTMENT MANAGEMENT

A smile can be heard over a telephone. The phone is one of the most important tools you have to create a first impression. Smile when you answer the phone. You may feel like a complete twit, but that smile will be transmitted to your client. Stay calm and deliberate in your delivery, no matter how rushed you feel. Your smile, and your cheerful, enthusiastic voice could be the nicest thing to happen to your client in her day.

Always answer the phone on the second or third ring and clearly state: "Good Morning/Afternoon", followed by the name of the salon and then "This is (your name) speaking". By using "this is" before announcing your name you display confidence. You are proud to be working in this beautiful salon.

The phone is a "selling tool" and should only be answered by an experienced operator. It is not a job to be handed to the youngest employee in the salon. That young person is too busy anticipating and fulfilling all the needs of the senior stylists to help their day flow as efficiently as possible. They don't have time to answer the phone.

When the stylist returns to her client, there should be absolutely no discussion about the content of the phone call. Remember salon etiquette is all about the client sitting in front of you. She has no interest in anything other than herself and nor should she.

One of the best ideas I have heard of for control of the phone, was from a stylist starting her own salon, which just happened to have been a beautifully created salon space attached to her home.

She was the only operator in her salon and she worked just three days a week.

She decided that she would not interrupt the time with her existing client to answer the phone call of another client.

Her phone was on "silent" mode and her message was thoughtfully recorded. She trained her clients to leave a message and she responded when she was free. Her clients accepted the fact that they had to leave a message because they knew the same courtesy would be extended to them when they were in the chair.

All that was ever heard in her salon was beautiful music and gentle conversation.

This stylist decided on all of the rules that would apply to her business, before opening her salon, the phone use included.

Another stylist had set rules about appointment times.

He also worked by himself in his salon. All his clients were told in advance of the rules and he never compromised one client at the expense of another by accepting a late client. If they were late by five minutes they didn't get a shampoo. If they were late by ten minutes they didn't get a blow dry and if they were late by fifteen minutes they forfeited their appointment. He had them reschedule their appointment. His reasoning, which I respect, was that he was not going to be made to run behind all day and upset the clients who did turn up on time because of another errant client.

His business ran like a well oiled machine, and I did not ever see one of his clients arrive late. He enjoyed his day and his clients enjoyed his expertise, and the fact that they were not being inconvenienced. That is excellent client care and salon etiquette as well. It's all in the way that the rules are explained to the client.

Most people have very busy lives and they appreciate their time not being wasted by having to sit for hours in your hairdressing salon.

24

THE COMPLAINING CLIENT

Stay Calm

Complaining clients are good for you. At least they come back.

She walks into the salon very briskly. Usually she has been encouraged to complain by her friends and that's alright for them. She is the one that has to front up to you, and tell you that you have wrecked her hair. She is nervous and she is angry to have been put in this situation.

Stay calm. Be brave! Greet her kindly and get her into your salon and seated as quickly as possible. Now sit down beside her and really LISTEN to where she is coming from. Don't take any of her complaint personally. Take it very professionally. Really listen, and maintain eye contact. Focus on her every word. Let her talk. Do not interrupt. When you are sure you understand what she is complaining about, you need to clarify her complaint.

Hairdresser: "The reason you don't like your colour is that it's too yellow, is that right Sue?"

Sue: "Yellow! I've seen canaries that look pale by comparison!"

Hairdresser: "I am so sorry Sue. We have a few alternatives to eliminate the yellow, and we really want to make you happy. Naturally there would be no charge. Would you like it done now, or could I make an appointment for you?"

1. Clarify the complaint.
2. Apologise.
3. Provide a solution.
4. Fix it as soon as possible.

Don't tell her how much you like it and don't drag one of your co-stylists over to back you up with false assertions of how much it suits her. Just deal with it and get on with your day.

Now I know how this feels. As a stylist you feel gutted and embarrassed, and you should feel this way. It helps you to never let anyone walk out of your salon when you really know you have not done the right thing, and you know that the client is not completely happy. If you don't deal with it before she leaves the salon it will get embarrassing, or worse still, you will never hear from or see that client again.

Do remember that it took a lot of guts on her part to come back. We should be giving those clients a big hug, and you should genuinely thank the client for giving you a second chance to make your first impression.

You see, that client wanted you to succeed. She wanted

you to make her look drop-dead gorgeous. She was on your side all the way, until you didn't perform. Now she is disappointed and as mad as hell that she has to go back to your salon and tell you she is unhappy.

Don't put yourself through this stuff. Learn your trade well and be technically competent and recognise and acknowledge when you're at fault. Look into the matter honestly and leave your bruised ego out of the equation.

25

CLIENT COMFORT

Snug As A Bug In A Rug

She got wet!

Almost drowned in fact. Water all the way down her back.

Those carefully penciled on eyebrows are gone.

All gone with that sloppy basin technique.

The shampoo area is probably the most important area in the whole salon. It is usually where first impressions are made, and it is usually the domain of the younger stylist in the salon who would rather row across the Atlantic than do one more shampoo in this salon.

Now, pay attention, because this is very, very important!

GOOD ADVICE GEM

Young stylists or apprentices as they are sometimes referred to, are the most important people in a busy salon and they give the edge to a successful salon's operation.

They need to be made to feel very important. They need to know that without their amazing attention to detail and the great care and professionalism they offer each and every day, the salon would just not perform efficiently, professionally and profitably. They are the core of the operation. They run the joint, and you as the salon owner are going to invest a lot of your time and effort in training these young people to do the small things extremely well. The attitude instilled in the young stylists is going to carry through their whole careers as stylists and hairdressers.

Your young stylists know in advance what is needed in every corner of your salon. They will anticipate the needs of the senior stylists and the clients. They are time managers and stock controllers. They are the efficiency experts and when they have a day off you should FEEL IT.

However, they do have to learn how to avoid wetting the client at the basin, or washing off her carefully penciled eyebrows.

The shampoo is probably the first thing your client experiences in the salon, so it had better leave a great impression, because if the shampoo and basin care are excellent, the client is on a high when she gets to the stylist.

I believe a shampoo should be performed in silence.

No tricky questions about what sort of a day the client has had.

Everyone has to be invited to shut up (not to talk), because in a lot of cases it doesn't come naturally.

Once the client is well wrapped in preparation for her shampoo, and her position at the basin is established to avoid getting wet, then the young stylist is going to invite silence by stating the obvious.

Young Stylist: "Sue, I am going to shampoo your hair for you now and I would like you to just relax and enjoy. Are you comfortable?"

Murmurs of assent should be heard.

Now the young stylist is going to perform her magic.

Silently.

A beautiful, efficient shampoo and condition is then performed without removing eyebrows, loading ears with soap suds, jangling bracelets in clients ears, spraying spurts of water over carefully applied make up or massaging with such force that the client is fearful of fingers penetrating the brain.

Comfortable, methodical, professional and efficient.

Please don't use the shampoo area for making up time for a behind-schedule senior stylist. Hanging in the shampoo position for extended periods may not be your client's idea of a good time.

Following the basin treatment, take care to comb the client's hair into her usual shape before inviting her to cross the floor to her stylist. She should not walk to the chair with a towel half hanging over her head or her hair slicked straight back from her forehead in a most unflattering way.

You could offer the client a tissue at this stage, just in

case she did get a little damp around the ears.

Some clients have the most sensitive scalps and cannot tolerate too much brushing or massaging. Just ask the question at the very early stages of your consultation with the client, to establish if they have any concerns with their scalp.

26

THE TECHNICAL STUFF

Get Educated

It is vital that a good hairdresser who offers excellent client care, should also have a very good technical understanding of hair and of the chemical processes the hair is going to be subjected to. Good technical knowledge helps prevent mistakes and solves a lot of problems for your client. Education is the key to good technical knowledge. You will find that the manufacturers of the products you choose to use in your salon would have a calendar of educational events that you should make the effort to attend. It is true that even if you learn only one thing, it is worthwhile attending. Keep attending these events, because you can never know it all.

27

CONFIRMATION OF APPOINTMENTS

This is so important for the running of a smooth and professional operation. Don't just assume your client is going to turn up for her appointment. A text message asking for confirmation is an excellent insurance against *no shows*. Most computerised appointment systems will have this as an automatic service.

28

IN CLOSING

May I wish you all the very best in this amazing industry you have chosen to make your profession. Hairdressing is hard work and you are selling yourself first before you sell your ability and devotion to client care.

Every day must see an improvement in your ability and your level of service for you to become truly proficient as a hairdresser.

I know that with each of your clients, you genuinely strive to excel. I also know that it is the times when we don't live up to our clients' expectations that are the true learning opportunities.

Unfortunately, all of us have probably had that awful experience of letting a client down by not fulfilling her wishes. It is better to strive for excellence at every opportunity, than to lose sleep over any failures.

As a hairdresser you bring a lot of joy to the lives of others. You can improve the outcome of your client's day by a simple blow dry.

This profession will be with you for the rest of your life.

Once learned, you will always be able to *do hair*. This will make you invaluable to your friends and also to complete strangers.

You will always have a job, no matter where you find yourself in the world.

A good haircut is universal on male or female.

You are set for life!

Your trump card for success within your profession is when you understand the true meaning of Client Care.

I hope you find inspiration from this story.

I would like to leave you with my Top Ten Tips for Client Care:

1. Listen to your client when she is telling you what she wants.
2. Resist the urge to talk about yourself.
3. Ask good questions.
4. Remember your client's name and use it often.
5. Leave your ego at home. It's all about the client.
6. Be honest.
7. Under promise and over deliver.
8. Keep good records.
9. Be technically correct in your work.
10. Always be kind.

And my Top Ten Tips on what not to do:

1. Do not talk about yourself.
2. Do not look in the mirror at yourself while you talk about yourself.
3. Do not talk to your fellow workmates over your client.
4. Do not ask personal questions of your client.
5. Do not talk about yourself.
6. Do not cut hair shorter than requested.
7. Do not talk about any other client to your existing client.
8. Do not talk about yourself.
9. Do not forget your client's name.
10. Do not let you client leave the salon with colour on the skin, around her hairline, or bits of hair stuck to her clothes.

I wish you fulfillment and success in your hairdressing career.

Lee Watt

ABOUT THE AUTHOR

Lee Watt began her career as a hairdresser in a small city in Queensland, Australia. The natural progression for someone of ambition in the hairdressing industry led her to establish her first Salon in that same town. This Salon proved to be a success. Ultimately, Lee decided to concentrate more on training, sales and management, allowing her talented pool of stylists to look after the cutting, colouring and other hair treatments.

After owning and managing two other successful salons in Brisbane, Queensland, Lee was appointed Queensland Sales Manager for a major Australian manufacturer of a range of prescription hair care products, eventually spending a year in San Francisco CA in the USA, setting up a hair and scalp clinic and retail outlet for this company.

With the experience gained in hairdressing, and utilising the principles of Client Care expressed in this book, Lee then moved on to women's fashions. She established a boutique for women's clothes and shoes in an up-market area of Brisbane, which thrives to this day.

11597229R00042

Printed in Great Britain
by Amazon.co.uk, Ltd.,
Marston Gate.